Sun Power

Louis Capra

What helps plants grow?

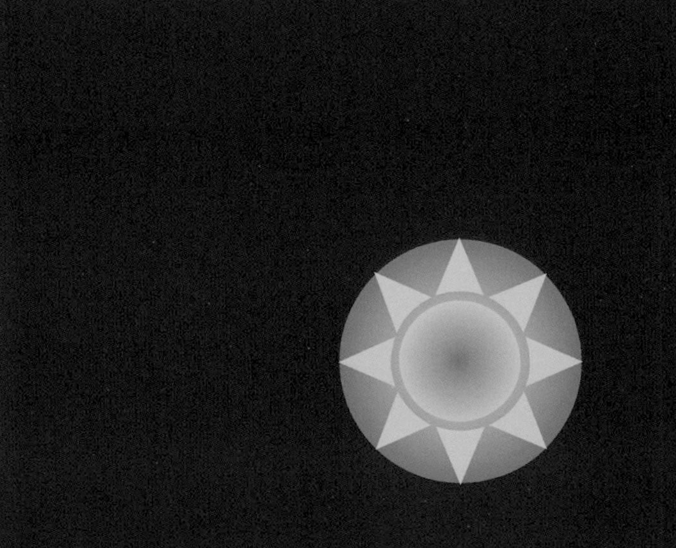

What makes this car go?

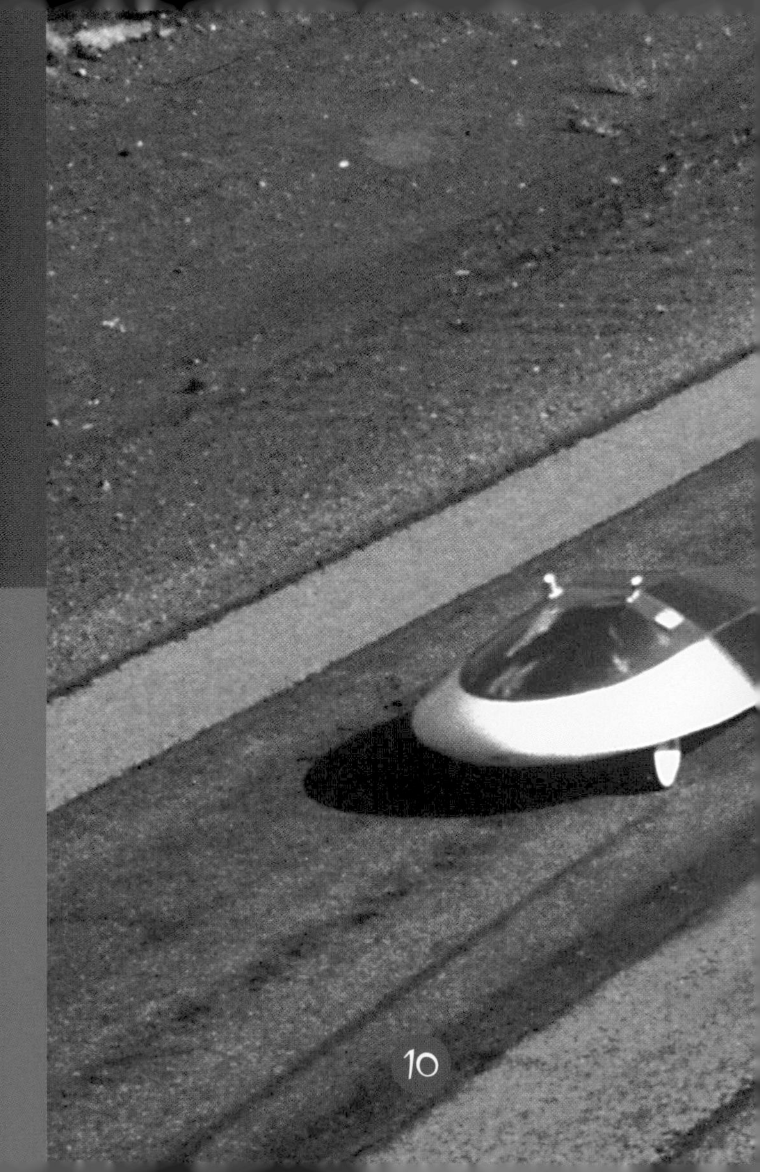

Sun power!

This car uses sunlight to make the car go.

PENTAX
WORLD SOLAR
CHALLENGE

What heats the houses?

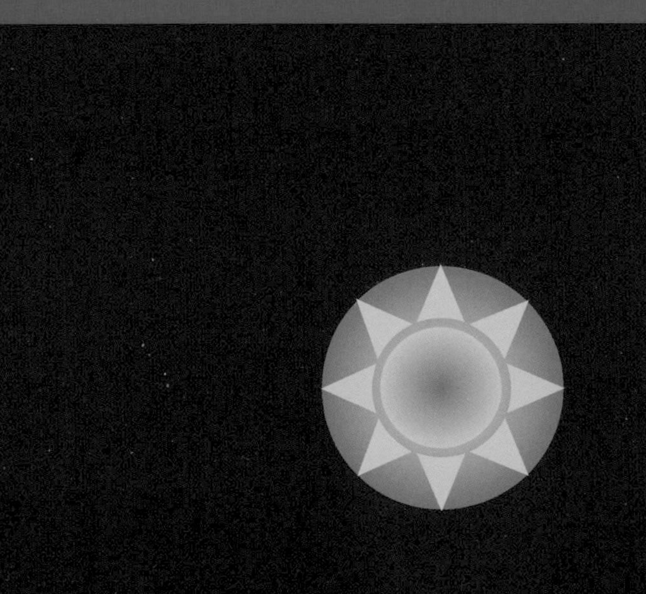

Sun power!

The panels on the roofs use sunlight to heat the houses.

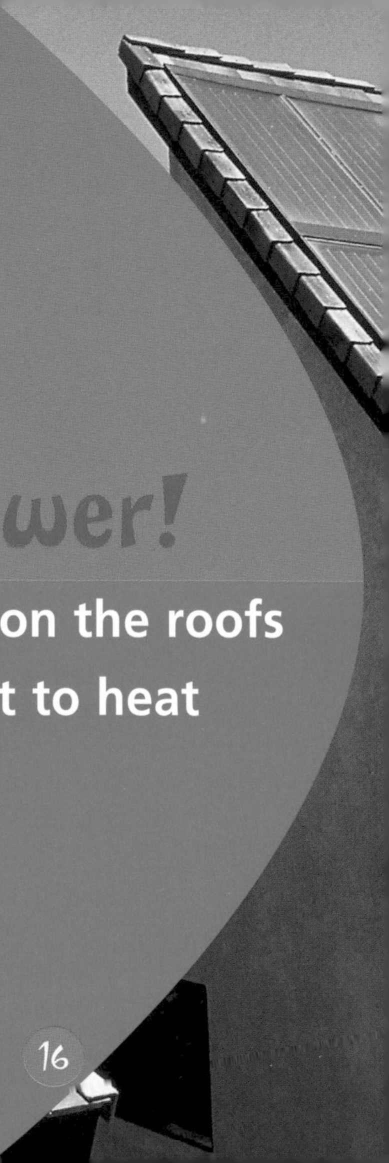

What helps dry the clothes?

What helps keep you warm?

Sun power!

Index